The poems in *Reckless Toward Blossoming* reflect on a transition that begins following an unanticipated change in the course of life and moves toward, but never quite reaches, a satisfactory end. Unexpected reversal always begins with shock and grief. But the idea of hope is embedded in the writing from the very beginning, and is, in fact, central to the progression of the poems. Hope is an immense concept, and there are many ways a person can answer the call it presents. The insistent, intentional pursuit of understanding and healing can be undertaken with a recklessness that isn't always a bad thing. Sometimes it's a type of salvation.

When Liz Lochhead, Scots Makar (the national poet of Scotland), spoke at the Edmonton Poetry Festival in April 2013, she said, "Never assume that the 'I' in a poem is the poet speaking." Poetry is a form of fiction. I hope readers will be able to "take part in the fiction" in a way that makes it theirs as they navigate their own perilous passages.

Deborah Lawson
Edmonton, Alberta
May 2013

D0824916

"The truth may set you free, but first it will
shatter the safe, sweet way you live."

~ Sue Monk Kidd, *The Dance of the Dissident Daughter*

"I am a slow un-learner, but I love my un-teachers."

~ Ursula K. LeGuin

Reckless
Toward Blossoming

by Deborah Lawson

 Frontenac House Poetry

Book design: Epix Design
Cover Image: Neil Petrunia
Author photo: Mark Zeltserman

Library and Archives Canada Cataloguing in Publication

Lawson, Deborah, 1953-
    Reckless toward blossoming / Deborah Lawson.

"Quartet 2013".
Issued also in an electronic format.
ISBN 978-1-897181-92-8

    I. Title.

PS8623.A938R43 2013   C811'.6   C2013-901357-1

Frontenac House Media gratefully acknowledges the support of the Canada
Council for the Arts for our publishing program. We would also like to thank
the Government of Alberta Multimedia Development Fund for their support
of our publishing program.

Canada Council   Conseil des Arts   **Government**
for the Arts   du Canada   **of Alberta** ■

Printed and bound in Canada
Published by Frontenac House Media Ltd.
1138 Frontenac Ave. SW
Calgary, Alberta, T2T 1B6, Canada
Tel: 403-245-8588

For my children, Vanessa, Owen and Devin
—still unfolding before my eyes ...

Table of Contents

Landscape Makes a Promise   9
Sometimes   10
Chase   12
Like This?   13
DiMaggio & Monroe   14
Sunday Afternoons   15
Touchstone   16
Nothing Worse   17
Turtle Lake: Grasshopper   18
Quilt   19
On the Bus to Grande Prairie   20
Goes Both Ways   21
The Lengths of Time   22
Lost Years   24
Game Theory   25
Altar   26
Eruption   27
Dutch Lake   28
Freedom's Gavel   30
Nausea   31
Drowning Together   32
The Boys of Spring   33
Saving Space   34
Dead Nun's Underwear   35
Pins and Needles   36
Her gaze keeps coming back   37
Four Ways of Telling Time   38
Caragana Perfume   40
Bullet Train   41
Beneath Bedrock   42
Not What You Expected   45
Moving   46
See this scar?   48
Frozen Liturgy   49
Winter's badger   50
Early Morning Train Passing   51
Ninth Summer   52
Concert   54

First Electricity   55
As all their brightness comes together   56
The Names of Hope   57
Map   58
Sing Spring   59
Five-Minute Manager   60
Kitchen   61
Terraforming   62
Night Light   63
Impulse   64
Old Growth Forest   66
Sideways   67
A Good Reason Not To Swear   68
Under Observation   70
Flashback   71
About Satiety   72
Dominion of Wind   73

Acknowledgements   74
Author Biography   76

Landscape Makes a Promise

I will give you green
in its hundred shades,
from the barest hint
threaded along the growing golden stalk,
to the near-black shadow
caught between thick spruce needles.
I will give you light,
the hard-edged morning's
etched exposure, focused
through dew's magnifying glass,
and the flat, direct burning of noon,
and this afternoon amber,
flowing ever lower over
the lush and liquid grid of these fields.
I will give you brushwork,
from sweeping and generous
to delicate and precise,
painting these contoured hills
onto flat prairie canvas,
where they rise
like a spirit uplifting.
I will give you the sound
of many wild hands clapping,
the echoing applause of the hills.
But when ecstasy
gives way to deep listening
you will recognize the sound
of your own wild heart,
echoing the heartbeat of the land,
the parallel sighs and undulations
of your own chambers of wonder,
a gallery where the masterwork
of this sweet landscape will live
as long as you do, as long
as your memory beats.

Sometimes

sometimes
you're lying in bed reading —
really *into* whatever story,
immersed in solid unreality

and then the house stutters,
intrusive shift of ancient wood
    cracks you into awareness
    snaps you suddenly
    back, story's last
clinging fingers
reluctantly disengage,
reality tightens focus
he's gone

and twenty-five years seem like
one long, convoluted, recurring dream
    the kind you struggle to escape from
    the kind you want so badly to awaken from
because you've had the dream before
and you already know the ending

it's not a good one

but another part of you wonders . . .
if you just stayed in the nightmare a little longer
maybe that freakish ending would
    spin on its heels
    spiral into
    sunrise surprise
instead of the ice-water shock
you've surfaced through every other time

sometimes
you cower from the curse of Friday night
with its emptiness casting a spell
so you can't tell the difference between
    waking and sleeping—are you
    awake in the derailment of your new life or
    asleep in the narcotic fable your sleeping brain

offers in its place, where,
for the space of two heartbeats, you think
    any moment now,
    the world will stop
    gyroscoping out of control
    and everything will be
    just like it was before
until, in the third heartbeat

you remember what it was like before

sometimes
the house shifts, a floorboard creaks
and for one wildly unbalancing moment
your compass veers toward the door
and you expect to see him walk through it

if you could see in a mirror
for that one wild, startled moment,
your eyes might reflect a flicker
of the original light that blazed out
to make him welcome

but the instant it registers
you're even thinking it might be him
the flicker scorches out in self-immolation
ultimate protection against
the slightest chance of encounter

and you thank God you didn't see
the death of your eye's light
    in a mirror
    or anywhere else
and even more
    that the shift in your heart
    echoes the settling of your old house,
chirping its relief
that his footstep
will never bother it again

Chase

Close to midnight. Sparse traffic
in the river valley. At one intersection
offset flashing lights stutter—
amber/red, amber/red, amber/red.
Along the switchback of Groat Road
my headlights trace diagonal streaks
across the shivering underbrush,
reflect the mercury flash of cautious eyes
hidden in unblinking watchfulness
behind the grey-leafed margins of the ravine.

The road—a serpentine sweep of solitude,
broken only by the hare's oblique leap
as she scales the berm, defeats her pursuer,
leaves the rolling chrome hubcap
coiling noisily on the concrete.

Like This?

Was it like this
I fit in my mother's womb?
Legs crossed, jackknifed at the waist,
arms linked around my knees —
perfectly pretzelled
into the available space?

Was it like this I floated, unaware,
in liquid impregnated
with the 1950s' Special Blend
— amniotic fluid, alcohol, nicotine —
gulping nutrition and toxins
all in one hungry swallow?

Was it like this
I began to be?
Curled and swam,
twisted, tucked and kicked,
tumbled and stretched
until my home,
without warning,
contracted around me?

Like this, decades later,
I find myself folded
into the disastrous space
of a life too confined,
drowning in the salty brine
of ambivalent tears,
enduring the wait
for that first unpredictable spasm
of explusion.

I exit,
gasping once again
to breathe
in an element become
suddenly foreign.

DiMaggio & Monroe

sometimes I wish
you would fall in love with me
love me unexpectedly
be utterly transfixed

then I remember something I read
about Joe DiMaggio and his
Marilyn

how he never forgave her
for her spirit
lush as her mouth
free-floating and teasing
as the billowing white dress

he loved her, of course,
in his conventional way
but his leaden expectations
weighted the hem
of her fabulous frock

and somehow I understand
that even if you fell
from the maddest of heights
eventually our not-so-famous love
would also fall to the ground
in a sad heap of white skirts
safety sewn into the hem

Sunday Afternoons

We used to make love
Sunday afternoons,
after lunch and the NBA on cable TV
or the replay of last week's Formula One.
We took our chances behind
curtained French doors that
didn't lock.

Then suddenly
every other door was locked.
We had sex, didn't make love.
The best you could make was
excuses.

And now, we don't even
make it
to the room behind the French doors.
Sunday afternoons, you
fall into a trance,
NBA or Formula One your soporific
drugs of choice, absorbed through
glazed vision. You lie
on the chesterfield, face fixed
on the flickering action until sleep
closes its wordless shutters
turns you away.

Touchstone

Today I drive out, secretly,
a day-tripper into my past, a vacationer
headed for beloved country
now lost to me.
Sold.

At field's edge a ditch cleaves the soil,
coughs up clotted clay into a berm of crumbly rubble
sown with rough dandelion and Queen Anne's Lace.
I trespass onto the only 40 acres I know anything about,
the last place I felt my feet firm
against the land.

I will stand until the future stops
whirring around my head. I will stand
—perhaps a long time—
until the willing black dirt
releases stored heat into my body.
Until I feel light,
let wild confusion permeate
and, strangely, soothe me.

Then I will give to that piece of earth
my gratitude,
'til now unexpressed,
for the grace of its grounding.
For the decades of peace it pressed
into my unaware hands.

I will hold out those hands now,
palms upturned,
and let the ceaseless wind of memory
stir
and settle.

Nothing Worse

in your jaw, that storehouse of tension,
the stillness of *rigor mortis* sets in
the planes of your face carry no
animation, just lips swerving into
    a public smile, curved to contain
    words you'll never speak

your body stands at attention, stiff
with good manners and civility
nothing indictable, but still
breaking all rules of engagement
       the assent you give to a stranger
       bare courtesy

a distance that severs all chance
of an uncommon connection,
you call my fire *anger*, and
pull away to protect yourself,
    but hearing it so mis-named
    brought the rage into it

you might have called it
passion, or even intensity,
might have let it kindle
some answering warmth in you,
    but we no longer speak
    the same language

Turtle Lake: Grasshopper

See the way you fold your articulated arms
into a prayerful posture?

Too human for comfort,
like a person dressing up as an insect,
or an insect trying to pass.

It wasn't my fault.
It was dark. You were so quiet.
Did you see me?
Certainly I did not see you.

No warning before I stepped on you,
bent your twig limbs into a travesty of flexion,
only a startling, off-balance moment,
a foot carelessly placed in a
familiar place made unfamiliar.

Still, the look on your armoured face—
can I call it a look?
can I call it a face?
—brought forth a rush of pity.

And though your life depends
on such a slender tether,
and though your body cannot possibly
mend, or carry you to a natural end,
I cannot kill you.

I will give you to the owl.

Quilt

plain of water meadow
interrupted by
fading snow patches
the corkscrew rivulets
of open water channels

the yeastiness of the earth
giving way to relentless emerging spears
an implacable rising
the original groundswell

everything buff and grey
a perfection of neutrality
backdrop for
the explosion of green
and green and green

the curvaceous sweep
of the highway
against the undulations of the land
hillsides narrowly threaded together
by the intersection of ditching streams,
where gravity enforces design

the sudden startling flash
of a grassy hillside
rimmed by stanchions of poplar
severely parallel along their length
branch tips bursting
into a praise of freshness

the cleanness of new growth
laying over everything
a joyously shaken quilt
settling into
its rumpled gestation

valleys, everywhere awakening

On the Bus to Grande Prairie

Just north of Valleyview
muscular clouds stretch
low against the earth,
bend over October's buttered aspens.
Highway descends into a bowl,
brimming popcorn of trees.

Golf-flake leaf litter,
zebra-striped birch trunks,
spacious field like a face
freckled with hay biscuits.
Cleared logs, a tumble of pick-up sticks,
beaver domes with their
whispered secrets of habitation.
Pale boulders in a marbly huddle.
Roadside shrines inviting the devout
to contemplation.

But the rocks themselves compel me
to devotion, more than the shrines
we fly past as the thread of highway
unspools, invisible ahead and behind.

They draw me close
to the taste of this land,
the way it merges into
the magnetism of
now.
The way it knows
how
to be.

Goes Both Ways

     just a magpie
     we say

iridescent feathers measure
her awkward length

     just a magpie

ungainly pace
raucous squawk, hops,
flaps, scatters dust

Magpie must
know our dim opinion
of her

     casts it back
flash of black gloss
posturing of purple
bright white disregard

lifts her clumsy
lumbering bulk with
unfazed grace, up to tapering
twig-ends of elm or lilac,
settles her metallic glory

bored
with our contempt

     Magpie looks down
     on us

The Lengths of Time
(A cosmological allegory)

From *The Canadian Oxford Dictionary*:
eon: the largest division of geological time, composed of two or more eras | **era**: a major division of geological time that is a subdivision of an eon and is itself divided into periods | **epoch**: a division of geological time, esp. a subdivision of a period corresponding to a set of strata

We postulate eonic movement in
an eternally trembling universe,
backdrop for a ponderous galaxy
in which Sol hangs motionless ...
or so it appears.

    Yet
our fixed, exquisite star is a whirling dervish,
our blue-green home less than a thought,
our days a bare
    blink
in eternity.

Within a vast cosmic lethargy
earth's hasty geology accumulates
mere billions of years,
against which fragile mortality
dares to measure
    a life,
stretch out its length upon a monumental scale,
and wonder

    how pain
can expand one short day
into an epoch,

how loneliness
can compress
an entire strata into the
space between two heartbeats.

If
one eon equals two eras,
then
the sharing of
one heartache, a life-quake,
may equal two versions of misery,
each with its own timeline.

And who is to say
which takes longest to pass?

Lost Years

so much is gained
when the lost years are tallied, added
to time newly found

the beauty of the daily
the willingness to exult in tender things
    each blade of grass, erect and shining
    springing up to meet the moment

the grace of laughter
carried on helpless breath
    the mirth of dandelion fluff
    snagged in a window screen

no mere concessions these
but rather, the unbidden celebrations
of a renascent future

Game Theory

Who Wants To Be A Millionaire?
Are You Smarter Than A Fifth Grader?

We're in love with our game shows
(all those genial hosts).
We love to guess—guess again!
We call out the answers,
get so many right,
can't tear our eyes off
the shiny trinkets ...
all we could win
if we got on the show!

Then the TV goes off.
We won't meet each other's eyes.
Jeopardy plays in our own living room.
No more right answers—
can't even ask the right questions.
And forget trying to guess.

Altar
(After 9/11)

If incense is the point,
    smoke rising into the sky,
    a sacrifice that really costs,
perhaps high-rise destructions
will suffice.

If not,
if it's about the silencing of voices
    entombed in secrecy,
    never subject to public outrage,
perhaps a discreet genocide
is sufficient.

Fuel for the altar.
The only way we know
to bring about change,
to transform humanity.

We have not forgotten
the violence of sacrifice,
    the need for a victim,
    the flash of the knife.
But we've forgotten
    why they were required to begin with,
failed to question
    the reason, the meaning, the need.

A strange compartmentalization.
Partial amnesia
in a dangerous priesthood.

Eruption

Given time enough,
and pressure,
given heat and containment,
the expectation of eruption
is in direct proportion
to the presence
of all the above
plus two human beings.

Dutch Lake

Do you remember
growing up as cousins together
in the sixties, the six of us
all wild and sunburned,
swarming into the box of the pickup,
clinging with lichen's grip all the way to the beach,
daring each other to swim across
Dutch Lake—*the lake with no bottom?*

I still feel the goosebumps of a child's
baseless fear when I hear that name:
Dutch Lake. Some said its blackness
came from a coal seam that ran beneath it,
east to west. But we knew better—we knew
it went down, down forever until,
like an Olympic swimmer executing
a flip-kick at the edge of a pool, it turned
and came up somewhere in China,
where all the Chinese kids brave enough
to swim in a lake with no bottom
knew. Just as we knew.

The thrill of that knowledge on the long swim out
to the raft—floating fixed and tangible above
the rumours—taught us to be brave. I thought.
But as years blurred by, faster than
a ride on your oldest brother's motorcycle,
the courage of Dutch Lake faded,
diluted ink on the pages of our childhood.

First, the obsession of a lost love overcame
your youngest brother, middle cousin, closest in age to me.
With his long drop from the Lion's Gate Bridge
and the kiss of a rejected lover
on Burrard's concrete surface,
our six became five. As he dropped
through his own bottomless anguish, was he
spared that moment of sickening clarity,
of realizing he could mend from all his wounds, except
the one at the end of that hellish plunge?
It was nearly a year before they found his body.

A short decade later your eldest brother fell.
With despair triggered by years of ambition fallen
into ruin, he fled to a distant field,
his final protest impossible to miss
in the shotgun's shout.

Invading the chaos, disease wracked your father's body.
They called it lung cancer, but his heart was imploding.
They gave him three months, but he wouldn't take them.
He gave up, died in five weeks.

So here you are, the last man standing. And I wonder,
do you feel the danger of Dutch Lake, its inky depths calling
your name relentlessly? Or do you trust in the safety of the raft
which—in spite of being a hard and dangerous
distance from shore—must, after all, be anchored to something?

Freedom's Gavel

She did not come with a smile.
She did not come with banners waving.
She held no parade.
Instead, she came furtively. Disguised.
A devious encroacher. The silent
partner in a conspiracy to destroy
my naïve illusions.

The heart that was broken
was my own. How does that
make me the criminal?
      Yet for this treason
      I am locked up like a lunatic.

Impervious to pleading,
indifferent to my needs for
explanation or reason,
      freedom takes me
      into custody.

Only now,
      now that I have submitted,
      Stockholm-like, to love for my captor
do I see
how profoundly
I underestimated
both
her cost and her value.

Until now,
      I'd not have predicted
      the grace of freedom's incarceration,
or known
that freedom's face to me
would be as the first sweet air
after a near-drowning.

Nausea

When I carried my children in
the shelter of my body,
nausea kept us company.

Then there were the births.

How is it that now,
with a death,
that same nausea forces
its company on me again,
unwanted guest in
the house of my body?

And no parturition in sight.

Unless it is the birth of
new life from
this one grown old.

Drowning Together

(For JH)

Until today I stood outside your grief,
knowing only with my mind
the travesty of that vast absence,
the silence of a 51-year duet.
You were so strong,
so dignified in your acceptance.

But today
    as you walked away from
the mound piled high
beside the grave
into which, later,
unviewed, they would lower
your beloved
    as you faced into
a wind as bitter as your
sudden loneliness,
strength faltered. You huddled
in the midst of your daughters
and wept a river that
swept me along,
smashing dispassion
in a flood of empathy.

And for a few moments
    I, too, struggled to keep
my head above water,
hoping we would all reach
safe shore   together.

The Boys of Spring

I open the door to the bedroom my young sons share.
Sunlight's last piercing ray slashes the carpet.
The boys shun their beds, sprawl motionless on the floor
    (hot air rises)
as whirring fan blades churn.

Their arms are outstretched, not quite touching,
an embrace   interrupted,
    caught in mid-hug.

They breathe deeply,
blankets kicked aside. The sweat of spring's
    first feverishly hot evening
    trickles
from their foreheads,
    skirting the nub of the ear to
    wander
into pillowcase creases.

Their relaxation,
    intense
as my love for them.

Saving Space

She arrives at the task late, as in other years,
but she has her reasons. She draws out the process,
believes this is the last time she will
undecorate the tree in this house.
She works alone, takes her time. Space
will soon be an issue. Each ornament
is assessed, then carefully
packed or discarded. Each memory
is equally regarded, as are the
ugly little hand-made trinkets
she can't bring herself to throw away.

Oddly enough, the kids never made
those paper chains, alternating
links of red and green,
smelling of Elmer's School Glue.
But still she is linked
by dozens of loops of recollection
to the years that unwrapped
around that tree.

One memory stands out— a boy,
ten years old, marching back and forth
in elation, head swathed
with camouflage netting,
the genuine army surplus helmet
a proud crown.
For ten dollars and the price of
listening to his yearning prattle in July
she had fulfilled a desire, deeply simple,
whose satisfaction adorned the house
with flamboyant joy.

The decorations of memory
take up no space.
This one she will keep.

Dead Nun's Underwear

(For NJK)

These garments—gifts to her,
then passed on because they still had
so much wear in them.
Such a shame, even a sin, to waste them.

* * *

Her body had been strong through all those years of fertile service,
hidden away behind the cloister walls, or in the halls of parochial
schools—uniformed from head to toe for instant recognition.
She worked hard, kept her vows. With her graceful rosary beads,
her grave, downcast eyes, she seemed to us
the epitome of submission.

How we pitied her, the virgin life-long,
imparting to us what we knew was a partial wisdom.
The things we could have taught her,
we wild girls.
Things she would never know. The touch
that blazes longing across the skin. Lips
soft as the wing of a moth. The sudden,
indrawn breath.

And yet, here I have the evidence
that brings swift tears to my eyes.
This dead nun's underwear.
The shell pink camisole,
daintily fitted and cut to display
all her hidden temptations.
The under-slips of fine lace and satin
that slide through my fingers
like the heart of every sensual memory.

And because I have made myself beautiful
in ways that no one sees,
except the lover for whom I dress, and undress,
I am humbled to understand.
She, too (in chastity and deep secrecy)
is one of us.
A wild girl
adorning herself for the secret eyes
of her own Love.

Pins and Needles

This tingling,
this nerve-pinched sensation,
    a physical intrusion
    half numb and half electrified,
shocks my mind as much as it impinges on my body.

I've had it investigated.
The doctors tell me it's
    nothing.
"Stress," they say, thinking to give me
an encouraging diagnosis. After all,
it could be something so much
    worse.

But these pins and needles are
    unnatural.
Flesh ought to be quiescent.
It isn't supposed to harbour a humming
that builds to a buzzing crescendo and feels
more like   fear
than anything physical.

I wonder if it's not something else.
Something even more
    dangerous, more
    significant
than disease.

Maybe it's my spirit, coming alive,
jiggling and rasping its way through
physical channels long blocked.

Maybe it's the blood of my soul,
pushing, forcing its way through
flesh almost dead.

Maybe I'm
    finally
waking up.

Her gaze keeps coming back

to the view from her window—
treetops, etched like cutouts
in a child's craft magazine,
multiple rooftops, their shingled colours
a receding geometry.
The sense of being
above it all, an elevation soaring
toward grace. And behind
the blur of rain's veil,
the beautiful privacy.

She perceives the panorama
as a time-map, two decades
of seeing what she
wanted to see. Though now,
with newly cleared vision,
with perception made accurate
by pain, the view brings her only
a measure of comfort, not quite peace.

Soon she will look through
different windows. She believes
the change will bring release
from the magnet-grip that keeps her
looking back. Still, the knowledge that
this familiar view will
dissolve into history
is swathed with regret,
stirs up memories of failure.

The transparency of the glass
becomes a mockery, the future
obscured, even through gleaming panes.
Like a one-way street,
allowing but a singular route,
the view locks her
in the past. She admits
that, in spite of the loveliness,
this canvas has become
an anesthetic.

Four Ways of Telling Time

I.   river

an undertow
ropes of water pulling waist, feet, shoulders
equilibrium in layers
while the cold whispers anesthetic thoughts
in a language you don't know
but have never forgotten

when the skin of the canoe shivers
pelicans mass, battalions of dominance
a quicksilver shimmering overhead
they will not take you
even though they have called you
    it is a loneliness of wings
    drenched with away

try to describe their flight,
their mass against the brunted cloud-edge
falling over versions of the future
stroke by stroke in chaotic orchestration

    II.   seasons

    within the oxblood frame of bare dogwood branches
    against the late spring snow, turquoise under sun,
    always shadow, purple in the corners, to bring perspective
    the wild texture of danger and uncertainty

    the predictable rhythm of time—
    tick-taunt, tick-taunt, tick-taunt
    the intelligence of restlessness
    and all the hours, inarticulate
    there is no name for this
    no exactness to label the hunger,
    the weight of all that needles you;
    trauma perches, a hawk of vigilance
    on the slim wrist of sorrow,
    all you will allow yourself

III.   stars

midnight spreads his metallic blanket
invites us to his starry light show,
deepest night show, telling tales
of a mariner's journey, sailors
reading the sky's mapped brilliance
fearing nothing from the dark

still, they breathe easier
as the pre-dawn sky lightens,
a tendril of scarf threading daylight's glory
crisp air filling an opening cup

IV.   faith

rigid as a standing stone in a holy place
the woman waits
in the captive attention of fear,
body stiff, face a pale mask
until—suffused with first light's sheen—
hands rise to lips, then spring upward
in a token of praise,
disaster once more warded off
in the outflung arms of morning

Caragana Perfume

Around the edges of the yard,
breeze jostles the caragana hedge.
Drooping hanks of slender leaf
shake loose their sueded surfaces,
unclump. Golden blossoms expand,
plump with perfumed liquid.

We reach with care
through thornfeather lattices
to snap yellow nuggets
from their dappled nests,
fill our mouths with greenwater honey.

Sun chromes off sidewalk puddles.
We breathe right down to our
summer-stubbed toes.

Bullet Train

Giddy with anticipation, I enter the VIA Rail station in this city where I've lived for many years. Not until the train is pulling away do I discover my mistake. The hypnotic clicketty-clack rhythm I expected is drowned out by a drumbeat of dread.

On the margins of the track, crumbled buildings lie open to the elements, spilling their contents across the sand. We gain speed. In moments, I'm hurtling into a desolate wilderness. Through grimy windows I witness a parched and barren blur. Waste and destruction stretch to the horizon in every direction.

Although I detect no people, I'm horrified to recognize the grisly evidence of imprisonment and torture. By the time darkness blots out these images of violation, terror has nearly extinguished my desire to comprehend this strange journey.

Nightfall brings new torments. Disembodied words assault my ears. From imploring voices of anguish, hopeless weeping and moaning build to a crescendo of misery. The merciful anesthesia of sleep eludes me.

Some time during the night the terrain changes. As the rising sun stretches pale fingers into the eastern sky, her pure light dissolves the cacophony into whispers, then blessed silence. Sparse grass and trickles of water trace a tentative course toward a stone-filtered brook. The train races on. Signs of cultivation begin to appear. Before long I'm passing through a lush and fragrant landscape. Birdsong laces crystal air. I finally take an easy breath.

Suddenly we decelerate, pulling into a strange station. I discover I have travelled a huge distance in a very short time. I don't know the language here, or the customs. I have no money, no friends. But as I step off the Bullet Train, an effervescent relief raises me beyond any fear of obstacles.

I realize I've just escaped from a place that, although well known to me, has been treacherous and violent, filled with lies and betrayal. This new city, although still a mystery, is about to become my refuge. Soon I will have a safe place to live. I will learn to communicate, make friends, find my way.

Here, I will find my life again.

Beneath Bedrock

"You need chaos in your soul to give birth to a dancing star."
—Neitzsche

Underfoot, descended layers
of leaves past prime.
The unashamed season
returns. We see the bones of trees
| shapely | angular | graceful | bent |
In sere simplicity
the aging year bids us
join in her exposure.

Resistance—our first response.
The word *old*—at best an insult,
at worst, a placeholder
to maintain our distance
from the inevitable.

Rocks fall on the mountain.
Always down.
Leaves fall from the trees.
Always down.
And the years that are behind us,
also fallen
into the irretrievable past.
We prefer to hide
their accumulation,
to deceive, layering brilliant paint
on a ramshackle building.

But the foundation is
laid. Driven deep. Anchored.

Tendrils of determination
force their way through bedrock.
A costly labour.
Slow. Painstaking.
Seeking nothing less than
wisdom—elusive, precious.

We are miners,
helmet batteries failed, driven to become
moles by the absolute certainty of
subterranean sustenance, food of
wisdom, unseen but scented,
perceived in blind assurance.

How far beneath the surface
it is found! Found by those who are
content to let the ground rest,
decay—perhaps, even, to moulder.

*   *   *

Everything is down.
It is all
down.

And in the darkness—no
dancing stars to be seen, no
joyful music heard, no
fragrance to lighten the senses—
we find, at last, that morsel,
the eating of which is so
pure that all other bread is
pallid, insubstantial, little more
than a promise
to which we are drawn
by the downward
force of desperation,
inarticulate insistence.

All else fades. The pain and
nakedness of former atmospheres, the
stifling, shallow breaths whose only
meaning was temporary, even though
their necessity was indisputable. They
no longer suffice.

Beneath the crust everything is
richer, denser, more concentrated.
Thin gruel of youth enlivens only
the transparent young. Its appearance,
its nutrients, are breast milk.
In these opaque depths,
the muscled meat of sustenance
must endure the violence
of tearing, must be devoured
with teeth.

Not What You Expected

you come to believe that grief
is simply an inarticulate professor
sent to teach you lessons
you don't understand, never wanted
to learn, but must need to know

words keep you sane,
their jagged precision a foothold
as you climb, their sharp edges
cutting away the unnecessary, sculpting
your upheaval into something useful
    a magnifying glass
    the muscular bulk of endurance
    a cup that holds your gratitude
    even the blessing of each singular breath

so you wait for healing, think
you will be better for it,
but as it approaches, its irony
is an assault. You realize
    it was only pain that kept
    the receptors sensitive,
    found value in the
    raw material of betrayal
something is now missing

this void is not
what you expected instead

Moving

They say that if you move four times it's the equivalent to having all your worldly possessions destroyed in a fire. In this way, my childhood was consumed.

The military machine has a lot to answer for, and war is only part of it. In the early 1950s, with the shadow of World War II still darkening the minds of military strategists, it seemed premature to let the enlisted men and women get too comfortable with non-active duty. No army can fight well whose soldiers are not prepared to obey without question. No air force can succeed whose pilots are not resolved to bomb or die. No navy can prevail unless its sailors, in the rush to embark, are willing to wave hasty goodbye to their loved ones. Loyalty is everything; best it should be given to the Armed Forces.

The result of this was a decision, made probably late one night after too many paranoia-laced intelligence reports, too much scotch and not enough sleep. Loyalty to the military would be achieved by making it impossible for enlisted people to become loyal to anyone else. *Move 'em. Give 'em ten months. Move 'em again.* The whole country was mobilized, and there wasn't even a war.

Of course, a lot of other things were on the move, too. The divorce statistics of military families began to show alarming movement, an upward climb so rapid and effortless that it belied the anguish that fuelled it. Functional illiteracy moved ever higher as the most notable change in the educational status of the children. Substance abuse moved, with surprising ease, into so many PMQ's that it became just like one of the family, for a lot of families.

So much movement. I went to eleven schools in twelve years (ten of them in the first nine grades). Somewhere along the way, Mum moved out. In the two years that followed, a succession of apathetic housekeepers moved through our lives. They were so unsuccessful that responsibility for our care and the keeping of the house was moved onto our own shoulders—three children, ages 12, 10 and 8.

The one unmovable thing was the word of my father. He was in the Air Force—a military man. If he said it, he meant it.

I got used to it. And at seventeen, with one year of high school still ahead of me, I moved out.

See this scar?

How thin its imprint
on the skin. A wound now numb,
forgotten pain of long ago,
and yet the trace of it remains,
as clear as this fine line.

Carved and colourless
tattoo of injury,
it writes grief's history,
a quiet violence, now faded
but indelible.

See this scar? Mute reminder
of previous invasions,
of skirmishes that breached
integrity, drew blood. And then,
of slow repair, increments of closure.

This scar.
Engraved invitation to our wounded peace,
hostility's razor blunted over time,
boundaries newly drawn. Just
a faint puckering along the edges.

Frozen Liturgy

Snowfall,
frosted filigree, shaped
yet ever changing.
Overlay of silver hangs
on bare-boned trees.

The night is at prayer,
a shimmering worship as
peace falls, solid as darkness.

This is the jewellery
of hallowed memorization,
a litany of snow in icy
rosary beads, slipping
past guilt to kneel
in the clean revelation
of grace and forgiveness.

A fitting adornment for the season's
long sanctuary of darkness,
winter-lit, burnished by the candles
of rest and redemption.

Winter's badger

      sinks cruel, dark teeth
deep into the shank bone
of summer's long, sunlit days,
      worries away, never letting go
until those days are gnawed
to the marrow.

But even winter's badger must sleep.
    Then,
patient spring pries open the badger's
cold midnight bite.

Hobbling, tentative but persistent,
she regains her strength,
draws out the days in a long and golden thread.

Bones knit.
Sunlight returns.

Early Morning Train Passing

Slowly you wake, cocooned in your sleeping bag,
secure in the knowledge that your tent holds
nothing more scented than your intrusive human flesh.
No bear bait, no enticements for mice, no elk aphrodisiac.

You stretch warmth into rigid muscles, feel the fading of
downy dreams, see solid breath. Beneath you a mere skin of
earth, delicate as a lace shawl on the shoulders of the mountain.
A million, million years of rock. A billion, billion tonnes.

The incense of morning rises like a question, hovers
at the rim of a day that waits like a promise—open, receptive.
On tent walls, the shadow of dragonfly, a levitation of listening.
You hear the brief buzz of her rainbow wing in the silence.
Your thought becomes the corridor of her flight.
Sunlight's invitation is a golden lily, poised
on the tipping point of your emergence. You get up.

And as your feet touch the ground you feel the tremor,
a throaty whisper that stirs your eyebrows as
countless tiny earthquakes clap together in the bedrock's
eternal foundation, silence torn by the blundering echo
of a long, lonely whistle. Steam will be rising from steel rails,
dew-drenched in the morning sun.

> This merging
> of wilderness and civilization
> is what the day brings you
> first.

Ninth Summer

It was always hot.

I don't know how far it was to Antoinette's house, but it must have been at least two kilometres. Since my father drove the car to work, we walked. Several days a week, right after breakfast, Mum would send the three of us off to the bathroom so we wouldn't need to find a public restroom along the way, then drag us off, cranky and lead-footed, to Toni's place. Four women always showed up for sure, occasionally a fifth. They had surprisingly similar voices. Loud and hard-edged, raspy from cigarette smoke, a baritone buzz punctuated by frequent, unexpectedly girlish giggles. Mum had the only real belly laugh.

Sitting around the pride of Toni's kitchen, her chrome and yellow Formica kitchen suite, the women began by giving each other manicures. They all had magazine-perfect fingernails, strong and beautifully shaped. The most popular nail polish colour was Sugar Plum, but Mum favoured a shade called Coral Bikini. Sometimes they affectionately cajoled me to join their ritual. "C'mon over here, sweetie," one of them would say. "You're growing up so fast. Soon you'll be a woman." Another would say, "Hey, why don't you let me make your nails pretty? What colour would you like today?"

As their polish dried, they dealt out a hand of hearts or gin rummy — long fingernails tapping, lipstick IDs on cigarette butts, cards snapping, tricks piling up. They sipped a careful cup of coffee. Just one.

Then Toni rattled open the cutlery drawer, brought out the bottle opener, and they got down to business.

At first I thought it was a beer-drinking contest. Bottle caps popped with the regularity of a metronome, a syncopation of snapping and spinning. Snap the cap off the bottle. Spin it across the counter into the stainless steel sink. The sound of my childhood was captured in those sliding, metallic clicks.

Every woman there could empty a bottle in four long, open-throated swallows, head tipped back, face avid with haste. I wondered if the point of the contest was to see who would be the first to down an entire bottle without swallowing at all.

That was the summer I discovered *True Confessions* magazine, and read about Cathy getting an "A" in chemistry after letting Mr. Shelton provide special tutoring after school. Or Linda, who almost killed her colicky baby with too much gripe water. Or, most baffling of all, Dirk and Nadia who "went all the way." What was that, anyway, and why was it so shameful?

When I got hungry I'd wander through the kitchen, past the dedicated card players, and slap together a baloney and mustard sandwich with sweet mixed pickles on the side. The women never ate. Theirs was a hunger of a different kind.

I don't remember where my brothers were; they just disappeared. Maybe they stayed outside, ignoring the brutal sun and the gritty lash of wind. I'd have considered myself lucky if I could have escaped to the coolness of the basement with a library book. Instead, I sat solitary in the drape-darkened living room with the television turned on, volume low, watching morning shows on CFRN–TV. I recall little about the programs, except that none of the elegant, cultured hostesses or their fascinating guests looked anything like the women in Toni's kitchen, and they didn't much sound like them, either.

When heat and boredom ironed me deeply into the embossed chesterfield, I amused myself with the notion that the faces in the next room were just elaborate masks, worn so the women could tell each other apart, because they were all identical. Masks carefully patted into place, with fingers held rigid so as not to smudge the fresh nail polish.

But it wasn't even remotely amusing to think too deeply about Mum and her friends—to wonder what would happen to them. Much as I tried to dodge the realization, I couldn't help knowing: nothing would happen. Their lives were liquid. They drank entire weeks one day at a time. Four long, open-throated swallows and a month disappeared. Two marathon gulps and the summer vacation months were history. Their lives were swallowed up, as smoothly and effortlessly as two dozen Labatt's Blue.

That was the summer I started chewing my fingernails.

Concert
(To Cindy @ the Sleep Clinic)

Night music opens with a waltz of breath,
then soft palate folds in, master of stealth,
to blast into basso profundo buzz, trip over burp
into a hiccupped staccato chirp.

Volume varies from whisper to shout.
Air, interrupted, refuses to come out
until, explosive, snorts a sudden release
into a fluttering sigh that fades toward peace.

Silence—a blessing—for the briefest of times.
Then gravity pulls flesh downward, pressure climbs.
Once again a bark breaks the ambiance,
seal-sounds, walrus-grunts, building resonance.

All hearsay, of course.
I slept like a horse.

First Electricity

starts with the sky
    in that indigo hour
  pure with star flicker, cool,
    unaware of power

       at the horizon, electricity
         thrums, crackles, shifts,
       strings taut wire of
        topaz glints

          flings an arched brow
             above dusk's velvet eye,
               lightning asks the wordless question
             fireworks reply

       imprint a retinal image,
         searing pheromones torch
       for an instant, then dissipate
        into ozone scorches

eyes blink, faces recompose, introductions
    close the circuit, so formal
  we try to act

    normal

As all their brightness comes together

all eyes on her
as she starts down the aisle

halfway
    she stops
tips her face to the sky
laughs
right out loud
then
    she gives a skip
and carries on,
joy ringing its anklets
at every step

in this bright sanctuary
the wedding tissues
stay dry in our hands

        he waits, a deep lake of calm
        as she starts down the aisle

        the sun of his face
            surpasses
        the light that sparks
        through stained glass windows
        joy
            irresistible
        as the pull
        of a rare earth magnet
        vaults to her approach
        he draws a breath
        deep as yearning

        his smile is a language
        that says only "Yes!"

The Names of Hope

I have a talent
for planting bulbs in fall
that don't come up
in spring. That spring.
And maybe not even
the spring after that.

Then, two Aprils later,
when all crocus expectations
have long since evaporated,
a thicket of slender,
variegated spears slips out
of the earth—surreptitious,
sharply silent, gleaming
in the pale eastern light.

The clustered evidence
that hope's other name
is surely *surprise*.

Map

Today I saw a young man
so beautiful he shimmered.
And I pitied him.

He has only a lovely vacancy
where the map of his face belongs,
faint border markings
to plot his boundaries.

He does not have your richly carved lines,
chiselled pathways of permanent revelation,
or the magnetic upward creasing around your eyes,
laughter's strong, explicit topography.

Of what use is the young man's glory?
Many would mindlessly follow his face,
but yours is the treasure map.

Sing Spring

the plaintive lament after winter's long somnolence,
the yowl that cuts the ribbon on the season,
the neighbourhood chorus that cracks evening's stillness,
>as feline frenzy
>finds the proper key
>to sing spring

and my two indoor cats pace, taut and edgy,
long to join the freedom of their kind,
to scratch in soil the tilth of chocolate cake
>find partners
>in their laudatory urge
>to sing spring

Five-Minute Manager

Alarm clock,
with your shrill and persistent beep
you shatter my sleep.
I surface from depths, reluctant,
    immobile,
except for the slap of my hand
on your snooze bar.

Give me five minutes.
Call me again.
Between now and then I'll have
    breakfast in bed,
re-heat yesterday's leftover events,
digest them before time's next
    imperative summons.

Your five-minute prompt tells
more than the time. It's
a measure of
    importance.

Those mornings,
when everything can't be
    tidied up
(crumbs brushed from soft cotton sheets)
I want to stay
    covered up
(wrapped in bed's warm denial).

On those mornings,
my five-minute manager,
I find you most
    alarming.

Kitchen

The boy tilts his bucket over the compost pile,
a frozen, white-crusted mound speckled
with coffee grounds, grapefruit rinds,
lapsed lettuce, carrot scrapings.
He turns the plastic pail upside down
clugs it twice against the poplar stump,
dislodges the last crinkled egg shell,
turns

to a house mostly dark. From one room
old windows glow with kitchen's gold
translucent as slabs of caramelized sugar,
their jewelled honey-light spilling onto the snow.
His mother stands at the sink
where

for so long, she carefully prepared meals she
could not eat, patiently cleaned up the discards
of days as her world whirled down the drain,
along with the grief she meant to
hide

from the kids, their blindness feigned
to ease her sorrow.
But tonight he sees she is
smiling—the smile of five years ago,
almost ancient history in his seventeen years;
the smile, thought by all, to be
extinct.

Terraforming

I am alone on the forty acres.

Soft wind hushes through the trees, a sweet heaviness of earthy breath. The pasture grass is coarse and deeply green, laid flat in places by weather. Where it's still standing, it slants stiffly, tilting in the breeze. The deep peace of solitude spreads over this field like a down comforter.

I walk further, leaving outbuildings behind. The wind plays in my hair. Silence deepens, presses its healing emptiness against me. Grasshoppers flit from one hidden perch to the next. Their *zing-zing* muffles the hum of traffic from Highway 21, a kilometre north. Swallows scallop along the edge of the barbed-wire fence, their roll and pitch an aviator's envy, their trim flawless. A green-black frog, teaspoon-sized, suns itself on a fallen tree. I reach out a curious finger, touch its glistening skin before it springs to another sun-splashed branch.

I've come to gather rocks for the dry creek bed I'm constructing in my back yard, but tall grass makes it impossible to see the ground. How do I expect to find anything in this overgrown pasture?

I close my eyes, allow relaxation to flow through my shoulders into arms extended for balance; I meander aimlessly. Under my feet, I feel what I can't see. There is raw material here, more than enough to finish my work.

With my bare hands, sometimes easily, sometimes with a wrench of effort, I heave out the stones my feet have shown me. I brush away clinging soil, an occasional scurry of ants, the husks of last year's poplar seeds. Leaving a trail of patient cairns in my wake, I trace a ragged path to a tangle of deadfalls in a dry gully. I choose one bleached limb.

After twenty-two years of marriage, this summer I'm single again. Gripped by stubborn urgency, I am determined to build something in the aftermath of loss. The search for suitable rocks, the hard physical labour as I pry them out of the earth and heft each one into my wheelbarrow, the fierce joy of gathering stones of healing from a forsaken and tumbled terrain—all are concentrated works of hope.

In this windswept field, which I've known for over thirty years, the earth is studded with offerings to my future.

Night Light

Froth of hawthorn blossom
pale panicles suspended
along an intangible branch
a lacy tracery linking
tree trunk to moonlight

Delicate windflower
in virginal shyness
submissive
to the beckon of her
bridegroom breeze

White lilacs
luminous in the dusk
flaunt their fragrance
taunt our dreams
of desire

All white flowers
are best known
    to the indirect gaze
tell their sweetest secrets
    to the night

Impulse

winter's long build-up   releases
as sap of spring
surges
in adventurous pulses
   flows
in relaxation of melt
    responds
to sun's embrace
first fleeting
then
more frequent, more intense
   finally
     radiant

all earth's animals breathe
   deep
     deeper
into the belly
as cool fragrance
tempts them
to open up, pull away
from winter's hollow longing
into a flush whose hidden core is
juicy
   sensory
     spreading
delirious with the
   impulse
of emerging life

warmth wantonly entices
abandonment
of snow's puritan covering,
seduces a supple reach
of naked stretching
   moves
     reckless
toward blossoming

and we,
like skeletal trees with
　limbs
　　intertwined,
call to ourselves
　the pleasure
　　of thaw

Old Growth Forest

Beneath this crowd of ancient spruce trees,
huddled close in prehistoric secrecy,
only small things grow. Deep shade
blankets hard-beaten earth seamed with root wrinkles,
hungry for the spare sunlight that filters through.

Shadows, flung across the unswept forest floor
wrap me in a tranquil cloak. Spruce boughs,
their hair tangled by the twist and frolic of wind,
toss a penetrating fragrance, the aromatic piercing
of needles both fresh grown and offcast.

I see eagerness in the nursling spruce, so determined
to win its place in this grownup gathering, to tilt the odds
in favour of young life. Each year, its lusty shoves demolish
another layer of brittle neighbourhood undergrowth.

I know each step of this rough journey,
traced and re-traced over my brief years, 'til now,
in the dimness of old growth forest, memory infuses
my feet, governs them as they thread heedless passage
around ankle-wrenching drops, deep pockets of leaf-sponge.

I plunge down a bottomless sensory well,
redolent of childhood and charmed solitude.
My joy, though immense, falls breathless
at the feet of the centuries impaled on these
strong conifer trunks, whose very dust is an incense,
dense and primitive.

No words are solemn enough. No music captivates
the heart of this green religion. To consecrate this ground
requires nothing less holy than play.

Sideways

We call it fall.
Leaves disconnect,
release without protest.
They fall. But
not always
down.

Today, they obey
intemperate gusts, are
yanked from their moorings,
twist into the unexpected
vortex.

No gentle drift. No
picturesque float. No
delicate settling.

They scud parallel to the ground,
whirl in the escalating dance,
dive aslant into dizzying circles.

As I, too, am sent
        ... sideways

falling for you.

A Good Reason Not To Swear

I swore I would never look
at a man again. "I'm done!"
I said, at risk of being
charged with stereotyping.
"Right now, those Y chromosomes
all look exactly the same to me."

The universe has her own
sly humour. Can't bear to see me
get away with swearing.
Before I knew it, there you were,
reaching your hand across my desk.
The handshake was just right.
Firm. Not too long.

And when my glance shifted up,
my oath, firm as our brief
handshake, began to wobble.
Just a bit. Just enough to
dislodge the screen I'd hung up
between my eyes and any others
that might be looking—really
looking—as yours were.

So now I've stopped making vows
that endanger my body parts.
Take my heart, for example;
seven beats are too many
in one second. Or my skin;
vascular advertising
isn't subtle, as rosy flags
wave in convection currents
of astonishment. Or my lungs,
plunged for a moment into
the vacuum of certain ruin
if not for their gasping kick-start.

But it was worst for my eyes.
"Remember," I told myself.
"You swore you would never look
at a man again. You're done."

And I am. But when I ripped
my eyes away from yours,
I swear,
it made a sound
like velcro.

Under Observation

sometimes, when you lie four-fifths asleep, your
mouth moves, voiceless against listening air
with inarticulate expressions
of *in*
    (hungry to taste what insufficient essential?)
or *out*
    (needing to speak what dangerous thought?)

your eyelids flutter   you mutter
   an incoherent phrase
   (not English)
then sink into that final fifth of sleep
the scimitar sweep of long blond lashes
hushed against high cheekbones
tapering into the haze
of five o'clock shadow

I cradle my drink in unsteady hands
memorize your contradictory body,
power displayed in a frame
of tenderness, compact, chiselled with
prison-bought muscles
   (Agassiz vintage)
still lustrous with a golden sheen from
your last Colombian trip

   wonderstruck
at this beautiful changeling
who's taken the place of the lover I knew

while I
       am
utterly

   bewitched
finally

      complicit
willingly
          caught

Flashback

Her hand hovers over
the fruit bowl
heaped with bright variety,
a luscious profusion of choice,
feast of fragrance.

She reaches for pomegranate,
ancient fruit of passion
heavy with rind, feels its satin
warmth, its comforting weight,
then turns it 'round, sets it down.
One swift cut spills juice
over the counter, reveals
blood-red cells, ripe kernels
displayed in honeycombed chambers.

She teases out the seeds,
fingers and lips heedless
of the burgundy stain.
Tart garnets lay their astringent
sweetness on her tongue,
a momentary eucharist
infused with the remembrance
that she first met her lover
in a room with walls the colour of
pomegranate.

About Satiety
(with thanks to Pablo Neruda)

Your love for life
    is the zest of lemons I lick from your fingers.
Your sweetness
    fills the room with the fragrance of vanilla.
Your mouth
    is the strong tang of ginger on my tongue.

Like a perfectly ripened plum,
you are enough.

Dominion of Wind

Your voice keening across the prairie
comes to me in foreign languages,
a whisper in the aspen thicket,
or heavily accented with evergreen,
your breath smelling of spruce gum
and camphor.

At first
I did not like you, did not trust your
movements as you stirred, or the clanging
as you rattled the bars of the branched cages
where you lived and moved.
I feared the dirges I heard at night,
moaning all the parts of a dead day's requiem,
spilling lamentation into the unfriendly darkness.
Even the owl, so wise and silent,
fled your urgency, swooping
low and shadowy, moonlight-chased, across
the open spaces of our yard.

No matter where I went, you followed, shook free
of every bowery prison, made fugitive haste
to stay proximate, arcing high over tumbled terrain,
skimming the plateau of flat country. Stalking me.

Or so I thought.
And yet, in this expansive, lonely land
you changed your speech, put threats away, rippled
through ripening fields, beguiled me
with a resonant song, an undertone
of excitement, a symphony in my lungs.
How could I not respond?

I open to you, take you deep within,
become breath of your breath.

Acknowledgements

My lasting thanks go to:

- Alice Major, whose mentorship and example have been instrumental in the creation of this début collection, and whose very first sentence about my poetry included the word "publishable"

- Dr. Jenna Butler, whose creative energy and engagement with poetry on a global scale are inspirational

- David and Rose Scollard, who—four years apart and separately—encouraged me to submit my work for consideration by Frontenac House

- Micheline Maylor, my editor, whose insight and experience have shaped and immeasurably enriched this manuscript

- the Living Room Collective, whose workshopping has helped me become a better poet and whose support has been consistent, generous and unflinching

- the Edmonton Stroll of Poets Society, for providing poets—both emerging and established—with a venue for performing their work

- the Get Publishing Communications Society for providing me with the opportunity to present my work to a publisher (and Cynthia Dusseault, who started me thinking about the whole rollicking adventure with her question, "Don't you have something you could pitch at Pitch Camp?")

- all the people who, over a span of decades, told me I "should write a book"—there have been so many of you, and I hope you know who you are

I am inexpressibly grateful to every one of you.

Earlier versions of some of these poems have appeared in:

- *Other Voices Journal of the Literary and Visual Arts*
- *Writing the Land: Alberta Through its Poets*
- *Home and Away: Alberta's Finest Poets Muse on the Meaning of Home*
- *Freefall: Canada's Magazine of Exquisite Writing*
- Edmonton *Stroll of Poets Anthology* (all issues published between 2003 and 2013)

Author Biography

Deborah Lawson is an Edmonton-based freelance writer, editor, communication consultant and workshop facilitator. An award-winning poet whose work has appeared in literary magazines and poetry anthologies, Deborah also sings in the soprano section of the Richard Eaton Singers, Edmonton's symphonic choir. She's an active volunteer with many writing-related organizations. She has three adult children, a daughter and two sons. In her free time Deborah enjoys gardening in her large yard, canoeing and trying to keep her 1931-built home from deteriorating any further. She also happily cat-sits when she's not hanging out with her own feline boss, Muzzy. Deborah's idea of perfection is a poet in a canoe.